Love / All That / & OK

Emily Critchley was born in Athens, Greece, and grew up in Dorset. She studied at the Universities of Oxford, Bristol and Cambridge. From Cambridge she gained a PhD in contemporary, American women's experimental writing and philosophy, and was the recipient of the John Kinsella & Tracy Ryan Poetry Prize in 2004. She now lectures in English & Creative Writing at the University of Greenwich.

Love / All That / & OK

Emily Critchley

Penned in the Margins

LONDON

PUBLISHED BY PENNED IN THE MARGINS
53 Arcadia Court, 45 Old Castle Street, London E1 7NY
www.pennedinthemargins.co.uk

First published 2011

Printed in the United Kingdom by MPG Biddles Ltd.

ISBN
978-0-9565467-7-7

ACKNOWLEDGEMENTS

Some of these poems have previously appeared in the following chapbooks:

The Dirt Glitch Land Alter Affair (Cambridge: Arehouse, 2004);
How To Make Millions (Cambridge: Arehouse, 2004);
When I Say I Believe Women... (London: badpress, 2006);
Of All The Surprises (Switzerland: Dusie press, 2007)
Who handles one over the backlash (Norfolk: Oystercatcher press, 2008);
Hopeful For Love Are Th'Impoverish'd Of Faith (Southampton: Torque press, 2010);

and in: *Quid, How2, Plantarchy 2, Intercapillary Space, Skald, dusie, 'in blossom atop reeds it flares', The Paper, Pilot* series, *Default, Archive of the Now, Openned Anthology, Cambridge Literary Review, Infinite Difference: Other Poetries by UK Women Poets, Black Box Manifold, Onedit, argotistonline* & *Damn the Caesars.*

CONTENTS

Why should I not utter it, why should I not make you
contemptible, before I go?
I'm going now.

— Ingeborg Bachmann, 'Undine Goes'

The joke of our time is the suicide of intention.

— Theodor W. Adorno, *Minima Moralia: Reflections on a Damaged Life*

STRUM / strum

— Ed Dorn, *Gunslinger*

Love / All That / & OK

for SG, AG & EC

You hide the emblem of your heart, no, shuck it off;
& yours is freely loosened, no more freely got.

Love is not gardened (i) ~ it is wild & gone to seed!
  Why would you close that fountain, seal it up?
    Only, wander, uncertain of your worth,
    Prized from the praise that nourishes a sap,
  & shoot your sidelessness into the natural earth
Where it might prove a splint for something tenderer to lean.

(i) 'Love is gardened, closed now to worth,' Michael Kindellan, 'Oh No'

POEMS FOR LUKE (2010)

I have been thinking

So is it only that, actually ~
Hey, this does make sense & I'm glad
to know the harbouring curling
kindnesses of worry don't make it over
too much. Because I am shouting
at you, silent, &
want you of course, but also have been thinking ~

Still, there's so much still not to be said
separately & from our different positions,
like a failure to meet here
or at any point

With me, but grateful.
I am only just for using ~ or causing that hurt ~
necessary because true ~ from this place but
always getting updates ~

I don't want to be
genuinely sorry
but am so ~ it is me involved
in yr life ~
no, it is her.

There's not much left, of trust or ~
because c.f. everything.

This does weigh heavy some times too,
sticks to things in thick air ~
& myriad chances, like returning back toward
the same Orpheic point,

but of course
I have been thinking!

About yr last email, causing
so much. About other things too, really,
I feel. & liquid becomes me ~
or matching what's said with pouring
to go down, come down,
one of us, any which way.

Yes I see per se, but vis a vis others,
yr treatment ~ so we mustn't be sorry.
There's other things always
to prove & care about,
cutting little holes in faces ~
deeds out of words.

O you mustn't be unhappy. You needn't. I'm for you
tho our theories differ so wildly
& despite absence~of~love.

& still of course I have been thinking.

Supper is done

It is the skeleton of life propping you up in you half~baked like you
at an all~you~can~eat restaurant, not like you where you just
had to not come to reach an end to things, resolution receding
in direct proportion to experience or paying or feeding off little
doubt~portions flipped over or fried, in direct proportion to you
not getting what you wanted out of him as he precision forks his
way out of any~thing you 2 could have enjoyed together ~

Meanwhile he has dropped something secretive onto yr lap, it
bleats its mouth open suspicious, you don't know what it is
to be used for, your upturned hands turn it over in yr lap,
simultaneously they break breadsticks as if these were so much
amitié ~

Important not to exaggerate this weak awkwardness after the fact.
It is a close re~run of a re~aired television episode you've already
laughed yr sides open at. Somebody somewhere's gluing those
pieces back on, somebody somewhere else hasn't got enough
money to eat let alone this much or is being oppressed for an
Idea. How to keep things proportionate despite super abundance
in our midst ~ represent emotion~crisis in art, naturally, but not
at the cost of thinking the world revolves around ~

Nobody half opens the door to see how the absorbing banquet is
doing ~ that devouring stickiness lying demands an audience of
somebody other than just you. Now it is decided he will simply
go back to the woman whose eyes close tight for him each time

he lies her down wanting. This means you have no option but to go home not with him, not wanting, not simply, & again scratch at yr difficult like it was an irritant of the skin ~ maybe try to pull it frm the root ~

Honeymoon After Tikrit (i)

Won't you run with me now, past all the acting up & brushing off,
    & push me to float down *there* & there let me alone for good?
Won't you, when I'm *an insufficient woman*, point out the errors of
    my ways, the trail by which my false moves has everyone *be-*
    mused, & not ablaze?

& won't you cup me in yr hands & drink me on the sands, & send
    me on my way?
Won't you trash me in my talk & tie me to the mast, sail past me on
    a rock, split me at a word, defend me at the stake, & stake me as
    your claim, beat me when I'm lame, ride roughshod over when
    I'm good again,
& won't you always be so *good again,*
& won't you do *all* this
    for me, darling?

Won't you avoid me when I'm making love to someone else's
    company?
Won't you clip my wings & post them home, won't you melt my
    ways, then go out & buy yourself a telephone? Won't you live
    with me & be my love,
    & won't you harvest me & all the pleasures prove?
Won't you combine me with the gods above?
Won't you season me when I'm *sweet*, spring me when it's meet,
    chase me out of hiding for a treat. Or a song.

& won't you beat the devil out of me?

Won't you beat that ol' black devil off my back?
& won't you send me back where I belong?

Won't you turn out bad & say you're really good & shade in all
the colours in between?
& won't you do all this, & more for me, darling?
& won't you wink me for a trick, slink by me in a trice, & dice me
into salad, spill me for a shoulder (& good luck), & darling,
when you're *bolder*,
won't you risk me in a bet & double me or quit, & win me for
the rent, & fetter me unblent;
Won't you blow me like a joint & throw me to the wolves & hound
me like a dog & fill me with yr soothing words of love, fill my
head with soothing words of love *forever*?
Won't you do all this, & more, for me,
Won't you, darling?

Won't you screw me on the rack & rack me on the plate & plate me
to yr knife & knife me into afters?
& wont you, after all this, chase me into dust & rip me with yr teeth
& grind me into seed & crush my seed to earth & plant the earth
to loam & wash the loam to river & make the sun to shine &
plant the shine to grow & dust the grow to down & fill the down
to feather & weather up the best & rest me now to sleep & sleep
a thousand years with me & more?
Won't you do all *this* & *this* & so much more
for me, darling?

(i) Keith Tuma & Justin Katko, 'Holiday in Tikrit'

A Final Sonnet (for Luke)

Luke sits lonely & upended in the forest. Luke with a b.
Poor Luke to be so querulous to life & talented.
He that in that year
had very done much things. But to dismay.
Murder would not have seemed beneath him
at a time.

The willful dissonances of Luke's prose c,
& sumptuous cadencing ~ all this
to prove in pieces, what. Life had not
the measure of him.

He who died forward, with dramatic flourish, was both
a famous lover & a foe.

The basic timings harmonize in thought ~
the gulf between, mocking. Alas, in deed, Luke was a fool.

Dear Luke, It's 5.15 p.m. (i)
All these people in a tube crushed in together ~
strange.
I write across the soft wires & the hard wires
& all collective unknowns
in a bid to guess that you're the other side this train,
& no one knows it.

The crisis in my head ~ it'll keep till dawn.

Till then I wanted you to feel ~
from where I scrooch ~ there is no blame
(eye~deep in someone else's elbow).
This city's musculature, it spits me out at Greenwich,
where I stay, feelingly, for news.

Till then, so long

(i) 'It is 5:15 a.m.   Dear Chris, / hello,' Ted Berrigan, 'A final Sonnet'

We've been indulgent / now I can see round corners...

... & the view, it doesn't look so hot.
Luke, it must be to do with the future.
Why did you leave me for all that Viennese junk
when there's enough madness in this London light
to last us both two lifetimes
~ one of each?

Luke, the way over this impasse is not Stuckism,
it is you + me; you missing me,
me searching all over Europe
for that week in Rome; our work on phonemes & translation,
when you sent lillies to put me off & bring me round.
O pho ney me.

It must have been the lillies that did it

The experiment was me trying where were you

That's what you get when you put your trust
in men like 'men' I guess, or 'B,'
to tell you things, mnemonics,
for the rhetoric of stickiness, who cnt,
& stick by them, who fail
unerringly, the veneration.
Look, it's like that house
over there, shut up
with all that love~neutral
plastering it on real thick…
shored up through e~waves. Sure,
it's very boring whoever
had to sit thru all them various positions
& read it must be sick

I took it for a "door" because that's what
the man told me. Tried to walk
through it. Couldn't
take your time, couldn't
take mine. Unannounced.

While the arch leans bilingual
& equivocal.
Not backed by police
or any kind of force.
So B's furry but not all that 'cute'
no more ~ an intellectual thing ~
Like small & pointy, but lacking
brightness, see? & I like buildings
that match structural intent wth design

In summer. Flotilla of scraps
pulled into remnants
by a dead pulley system.
B is right, straight, & points (i)
his dick into the crowd.
Don't hype up sympathy
for laughs, we cld do this
feelingly if our guts were only
in it, not the cat.
Well, hey, who's counting
whose failure to be integral, honest,
whole. The sign said
for belief go right
& right again

(i) 'I'm free, right, and point a gun,' Catherine Wagner, 'everyone in the
room is a representative of the world at large'

You jerk you didn't write me back. (i)
& when you did, yr smile was Cambridge~shaped, judgmental.
I'm sick of all you bourgeois boys ~ who haven't read Catullus
or understood him ~
so I think you into the same shape,
& knock you into the same size,
like this & this & this.

That way, the next time you come in the room
I'm primed & ready with my gluegun.
To wipe up tears & spill the beans,
to make it so much worse
& arm you to the teeth wth all my paranoia,
O lovely paranoia; I give it you freely.
Go fuck yourselves ~

(i) '[Sonnet] You jerk you didn't call me up,' Bernadette Mayer

Luke, I can no longer stand you in thought or word or deed.
Your neon lego hieroglyphics turned out to be trash,
or worse, a monument to someone else's love,
i.e., yr own.

All I want is to return to Rome.
I'll dig out that figurine of the Madonna ~ the one we hid the
    money in ~ & stuff tears
of remorse down her throat.

(I need to feel right now how others have suffered
as I suffer.)

Deprived of all visions. Man, it's taking a long time to wake up
out of this yoga pose. Relaxation *should* be the same as praying
or communing wth Magdalena
about her centuries of bad PR by ~ guess what! ~
clueless whores like you

God bless you Luke. You were the only rat
that ever really took me to yr hole.
Nights run into days & yes I wish yr new wife well.
The weather is hot, I'm taking the chance to fan up
on my Latin & fling long speeches into the air
to an audience of just me & (now) this.
Meanwhile, traffic's at a standstill; London mobsters harangue the
    people
outside my window.
I told them to shut up & they got mad. Don't they realise
there's more to life than dying & drugs
~ tho I couldn't tell them what.
Say sorry.
Sorry.
Well what d'you do it for then?

Not home to myself this evening, nor to anyone this morning,
regretting how,
O Luke, I had a brittle 'scape!
Love's sweet brine disguised in a crab claw
nearly plucked the *big secret* out of me.

Now all the world's like a long hard drive from Greenwich to
Topeka.

Won't you hang on in there, Luke?
I'm seasick & the room's
escaping

O stayer~putter, slain champ
on the bright and verdant field
of love. It's 7.22 a.m. I can't sleep
frm the thrill of thinking over
to that Unionized State to find myself a boy,
a real live accent, to Unionize wth. Jamie
shown it all to me last night
on a graph: first the buzz of the sexual feat,
then a slump here & there ~ well you get over it.
Meanwhile back to books.
Yes it will be *then*. & really I feel now
I can forgive them silly boys for their exhausting parabolas:
poor brave lonely fighters
on the bright and verdant field of love

You're such a flake ~ I can't ~
with you no more. Nor any
kind of flavour ~
(tho the days are ice~cream
hot & I've nowhere to stick
to.) Besides which, when you don't
write or text or gallop over
my heart
I read it plain as academic writing ~
but more dull. Why can't signs
that lovers make be read? I don't know
why can't they?

Then plainly say "I LOVE YOU"
& the sonnet bangs awake

Avec fond memories

The would be falling out of joint
loosed among curbs; the light thoughtless
slinking.

I am here
tho Marilyn was murdered
& the labels they stick on things
~ perverse!
'Radical' for that same old worn old habitude,
'Kookiness' for such pricks.

& the thought of smiling, freigeist you,
trundling through yr mind
missing / not missing
that I love ~

just not to come anywhere near

Ain't gonna work on our farm no more

I mean, our garden ~
because, yes, I promised you annihilation,
no neat fountain / belonging...
While you sucker~punched me wth an ancient adoration,
enough to peel the frescoes off Vesuvius' walls. Then ~

Luke, you *should* be worried.
2 days wthout a word
now we're supposed to be ensnared & fallen:
a silence that puts mountains & deep woods to shame.

Not to mention this latest trick of stumbling amidst mountains &
deep woods !
cruelly timed to withdraw frm the fall out

which is this: a falling out & off & over
happy you

POEMS FOR OTHER PEOPLE (2009/10)

For Susana Gardner

What   possible   language can we   with your small o (o) &   my,
which is suited,   Is it a very very suited,   Tho the air
is not so much crisp where I write   How many thousand miles
frm you   I think it still a (seminal condition) we must might
        share ~   A spoken to, or from ~
A small you,   a duty to speak,   not to speak   To o to mouth
& make others happy   To write to be frward   A witnessing a from
a to ~   You airing the bright markings of others
'My strangely dependent on what those o t h e r eyes witness' (i)
        As form must surely dictate
Is there a   wayto A many   to get away   from
as I once hoped   We are all of us due   the makings
of our own waystoo

                                ~ Now I dnt no.
What must signify then   a beginning for us
in a new way, a now way, a vry vry frward & happy ~ I'm here
I acknowledge
        an entry promise marking,   a subject   solely
an urban forest
unfussed & unused

(i) Gardner, *SCRAWL* Or, (from the markings of) t h e s m a l l h e r(o)

For Seaton (after Ashbery)

The screen of supreme good fortune is carried in yr eyes, yr earth, it
is every~where wth you. These things: here a cloud stencilled into
the mist, there a small bird singing, could not be seen or heard be~
fore you wrapped me in yr skin blanket, called me yr own, & even
definite~ly one. Curved, I became exact & smiling

His
Absolute
Smile
Into
A
Celestial
Scream

ever melting in a shape, the most arbitrary of surfaces. Had been
my strategy to meter out exact desserts to people from a wilderness.
Whoso cares about denials, & wanted things, & least of all poetry. It
costs you but a kingdom of hurt to be weary, yes, & vaguely at

He
Traced
The
Green
Paths
To

conclusions, when the road divines in time, you take the one that's

not ex~hausted, to the wonder of flowers. Rose~centred &
fore~stalled, we wandered without purpose in expression of each
other, & from

She
Asked
Forcibly
Unhinged
By
Love
Quite
Gaga

& of a hue. Surely the trees are for each other too. Their greens sub~
merged & shadowed wth the corner of no evil; their defenses in the
rain: some lucky thing. Forestry arranged by providence to shield
us from our needs, all shot up now & jostling~virtuous

Yet
And
Would
A
One
In
View

of nothing. Which by any angle is a serious compulsive truth. The
crowded shapes, the shadowed play, the gotten up &, in fact, truth
of

Two
Faces
Glued
Fast
To
Each
Other
Permanently.

For Josh (after 'oooo the air is full of thought')

The air is full of thought tonight.
So sure, that my distance from you keeps me thinking that you
+ me wld make some kind of meaning in this emptyish universe.

Apart from nothing else, the aforementioned stars are out
& lie themselves apart
& light some way to distant disappointment /
constant as lovers.

The future *may be* burning or it may be very wrong. Talking
about it all the time won't bring it back.

And did I mention, sweet human, yrs is the only plaything among
sublime constellations that aporia means circumstance / notletting
is anything but gentle?

The imperialism implicit in all this is very hard to swallow,
very hard to take.

& who talks about the soul
amongst the world's souls anymore? Tho this catatonic accident is
sure / lovely, to ascribe purpose to it or cause is surely to provoke
deific discontent
when the days know nothing of elements, or higher purpose,
but are active forward now in a bright drive that will release above
our heads.

So do nights come forward like forgotten substitutes
once our heads be done;
& guide our hands together, to the pump of sleep ~ miraclulous.

from HOPEFUL FOR LOVE ARE TH'IMPOVERISH'D OF FAITH
(TORQUE, 2010)

'Content~Specific' (i)

'I look & look again'; (ii)
This language hath no 'ham' innit;
It hath the least epic infinitudes;
Nor loss of nerve, nor lasting incident;
Nor isn't the least line of an oceangoing barque.
It is a leaky vessel; a ~~~~.
Last time 'twas read
This language dofft bright & girdles towards
The Centric Orifice,
Waves (hi mom!) to the crowd,
In which a foreign nurse who gives you head
Turns toward the megafone to speak,
Her yellow crunches you; she doesnt
Trust tumescent judgment at the time;
& you are given 900x the right dose of prescription.
Yr prescription is to eat, shit, breathe out poems
For the day 900x per day 900 days total.
Yr inscrip~tion oozes meat out of you:
'Tis to avoid such pomes, whole books even;
Reminding of that place which made you
Yet which you needs must shun.
It is a cause of judgment / later on

A trip to ~~~~~~~ / later still a vision:
~~~~~~~ barfing through his own tower
Lists of the things he'd auction off like Bones & Gum & Shit
For all of us to eat
Later.

Yet still you press for worldly stature only,
& still the world pursues Jug Jug for an excuse
T'excise the finite, the only 'it' that we can grasp,
The ~~. I'm loathe to use the word 'verisimilitude'
& everyone will make each to their own.
The peops read want they want to hear NO MATTER
WHATS ACTUALLY PRINTED

(i) Peter Barry, 'Allen Fisher and "content-specific" poetry,' *New British poetries: The scope of the possible*
(ii) Loose translation of 'I looked and looked but I didn't see God', Yuri Gagarin

- *My notes*
- *Notes about me*

But when I did that, when did I do that, I never once did that in my
Life Apart from OK that *one* time when that one time I called you a
~~~~ When I voted for you I gave you my vote I showed the
people The insides of yr gleaming fishheart / yr trouble with love /
all that / & OK but you take my money to Chinese bookie,
You flagrant choice, you squander & you beat that man
with pockets Till he die, really, crammed with all those bits &
pieces you no longer recognize
Or want, & so I have to ask: WHAT ARE OUR DIFFERENCES
WHAT ARE THEY ARMS & LEGO PIECES because I like you
Love you hate you, most of all I not regret nothing
'xcept for those "sexual ambitions" & the strobe politiks
The fuckups in Kabul Yr Chinese power tool. (i)

& did you use yr tool out there & was it hot slash
very successful

(i) Josh Stanley, ed. *Hot Gun!*

Perhaps Other Reasons

That cat gut you've inserted through my mouth,
It travels down my spine, fires & tugs
With every movement, 'specially in my loins ~
It is the fruit of all seasons; a bird
For every journey ~ on each vital organ.
It has a tension you wouldn't believe, a ssssssspiccato
Belonging to the '60s. I mean the 1660s.
It is a little heinous corpus when I
Bend under. If you squared it with the up stroke,
You might smooth things over for a while ~
At least till I return to some other
Decimated breeding ground where the mood
Is fertile & the land more perchy.
Such times are tough, & I get easily strung out.
Also, I find with every era that goes by
This little throat gets less & less tuneful /
More grating to the ear. I hate to catch you
On~the~wing for such discussions.
& there are perhaps other reasons why
It's not the best idea

To his Uncool Mistress (after Marvell)

Had I but half a wit & space in which
Personal ambition didn't saturate everything
I did or sought to do; were I a man,
For whom love studied & love unattained was less
Vivid, resounded less than the *real thing*;
I'd sit & think & walk & pass my days
With you in true mutual bliss. We'd be
To each other the pearls & rubies I hunt out
In books & hoard for my own mind's sake. I'd fancy
Myself less a complainer, a hungerer after Renaissance
Fashion, that needs no real finishing from you
~ except as a prize worthily won; a jewel
The chasing after which, once gained, gratified
My seedier parts in self~intoxicating
Fantasy ~ my heart might really grow.
& never mind the Flood, we've save *each other*
From this world's weary transience.

I'd care less for yr eyes, yr face, yr figure
& the parts all vegetable loves sustain,
& try to offer you instead the rate
At which you should really be valued. For lady,
Love should be exchanged only for love. (i)

Alas, when I had all eternity
To chase, to muse, & wonder at my own
Self~worth; to seek for higher things whose sheen

Might give me that vicarious glow I crave ~
That which might make me look *really good* ~
You gave it up. & in so doing spoilt
The game in which you *were* the game, & I ~
The hunter, fainting after you, foot~sore
& heart~depressed with weary hunger. I
Would have been the only worm to try yr long~
Preserved virginity. Imagine my
Surprise when, with a light yielding, (ii) you,
An amorous bird of prey, turned to me with equal
Hunger & a need to share such love~
Pleasure on a level footing. The tamed
Grown tamer! No, it couldn't be. Your little
Ball once rolled & offered isn't quite
The same at all.

     Thus I alone now face
Those gates of life, content myself with their
Impressive height, desire to be the one
Brave lover~of~himself to try
To penetrate their mystery; conquer,
Or to still die trying

(i) Karl Marx, *Economic and Philosophical Manuscripts*
(ii) William Shakespeare, *Romeo & Juliet*

The Triumph of Misogyny

The theatre was very crowded, very late. First you want them to
jack off to the sounds of yr own pleasure, then you decide yre in no
hurry for yr will to be so adhered to, so you guarantee beauty in
Some Other Place. From behind the curtain the director is shout~
ing obscenities at the displaced starlets; there's a flurry of feathers
& tears. Nobody wants to see the mascara drip on the floors under
long~legged, weak~willed performance dolls; not when they've
been paid to sing & just shut up.
When I wake in the mood of a crab, disguise finally off,
will you comfort me with yr salt water & walk wth me sideways? (i)
When you realize yr other love, who's not even willing or the one
yre after, I'll laugh so hard at you my shell might just crack & fall
off. Then where will you be: you and yr long~dead poetry,
crying into yr textual apparatus ~ defunct apparatus ~ yr intended
interpretive activity. Huh.

I'll be the one dancing in the chasm that opens between sleeping
lovers ~
& what they wake to (ii)

(i) William Shakespeare, *Hamlet*
(ii) Marianne Morris, 'The Auction'

from SOME CURIOUS THING (2009) (i)

Studies have shown there are 3 different
genres of happiness: basic / sensual;
connectedness / eudemonia; & higher
purpose. Curiosity kills which of these.

Past Filmic Tense

it's said that whatever happens in life – desire consciousness self-
consciousness alienation dread – is really struggle of recognition.
Mother was there *for* baby, just not *with* her, or *when*, & then e.g.
taken in all this to be a product of particles

maybe as each cloud now passes overhead, they are the same
clouds, though different, just as we get a second chance, now,
sometimes (to commit the same error over again). This is what we
might call: marginalia

(Sense-Certainty, which starts out from the Here & Now, & deals
with the This, the particular): London Paris New York LA you me
Unreal

my presumption hooked up to your presumption e.g. Euridice seri-
ally let down by one she loves – dragged backward through alterior
arches – in perpetuity hoping. Temperament flakes. Lost hillside.

Ridiculous struggle. Acquiescence expected

the rules (of film noir) dictate that the female is predator even when
she is incidentally nature

(i) A rewriting of Joan Retallack's *Memnoir*, Peter Zinovieff's *The Mask of
Orpheus* & Hegel's *The Phenomenology of Spirit*

the *throwback* to the tunnel }from which
                              where you emerged recalls convenience.
In sharp memory Euridice's really a cipher, & the arch is a tongue
of weakness, the fault of belief. Believing where we cannot prove.
Proof to each shout of gratitude

the child recalls all this &, generationally, the part of her brain
where memory burns heats like a glow-torch. Meaning to see fire.
Come in curiously – there must we seek other ways

(Perception which may involve deception & / or reveals the contra-
dictory nature of awareness of world)

otherwise one could ask at any moment e.g. how is the hero
troubled by such a detail – training or bodily – & are we alone? (Is
such moment really of weather, or the result of mirrors.) Says the
Orpheus cipher to the Euridice substitute: why do you demand so.
What, is the same story not always split into different branches,
each absorbed trichromatically by eager, retinal cones? Each, brazen
on the moist surface, each clanging on the dumb shell

say there isn't an arch of memory merely the mode *through which*

& we can see back to (the Understanding which reveals order, regu-
larities & organization, i.e. the) one before this one

if e.g. in the past 30 years it's become accidental to pay more heed
to nurture than nature how unlucky the heroine / base matter of
our story, one that could so easily have been avoided, if different
seeds had been sought to react, etc., different logics of myth

but it's really too funny to think so differently; how one thinks on
such occasions yet feels suddenly on others; & to touch through
eyes, as in water or air, things swept whole into the stream

e.g. can sunlight be responsible thus for this shimmer, this photon-
dance? A beam in darkness: let it burst out of its language to com-
fort our gloom

come quickly the idea, leave your building behind you
come light without memory come come come come

While the past 30 years have swept by some daughters have lit up the details of memory with something like gratitude, prepared to repair. Now we are gratefully forward & bursting sweet violence out of history particles

doing her best to restrain lips she points to the bridge of necessity, silence on some other arch, doing her best without song

though Certainty of the Self may be lacking, may be out of this shot completely, the angle for freedom, & so, in a calm, clear voice...

here the arches may narrow, here, widen a little as if crowds con-
sciousness contrast or fear may be taken as a result if not through
them. The songs are both screams of passion & duets for distance

the brain repairs back to the walls of memory, green shoots flow
over the walls & the subsequent song may be either of victory or
warmth. Personal

observing reason which includes observation of nature & of self is
engaging (then) now in ambiguity & a range of genres which may
bring happiness lightly or may be in droves

less a port from the storm, more stain and stress. & it's super being so human, as in the body is made of the (past) – as curiously we differ from nature – might we not live than with reason (the many creatures depend) might we not clutch at gold rays in the bath

some may see at this point some point necessarily Actual, or set down in words. of rational self-consciousness so much is unseen though willed

(in selfish pleasure, in morality, we see so self-important)

Past Mythic Tense

how to present the phenomenon then? he who chose chose wrongly
& in doing our limbs are both crystal clear yet entangled

given the diversity of forms: to drop gold in the bath, to take noth-
ing of ethical wonder. the sections we carve, as removed from the
real as a sci-fi future, to say nothing of Medea

the soul branches out – we are entangled – the mother too comes to
the same point over nervously

(The Avaunt Garde)

speaking in logic (or Greek) where nothing's divided everything's
dug up out of the dirt, bomb or butterfly, but such dirt gets stuck
(like red paint) under the nails & the world after all is not for such
violent admiring. the archaelogical point may be us at the drinking
bowl us as the clouds part us offering ourselves up to ourselves in
graphic violence.

to get the beauty of it hot

otherwise one might have to ask something as vague as when I
write down my dreams – what fractals mean what --
Espressos for culture. tubebombings for resistance. subdivisions of
the Age may bring Reform, or they may just dissolve to Terror.

Curiously a hero fakes a discovery of poetic significance

Coincidentally Euridice flows into a wall of fire, an outburst, a
starling for morning

Leaving her fake birds clothes behind she flung at the wall & was
vaporized

At that all her words got replaced by signs   →   →   →

from WHO HANDLES ONE OVER THE BACKLASH
(OYSTERCATCHER PRESS, 2008)

Waiting

to force these intensities to a shape, to burst
or dilate. Body without cause, so detailed, so collate
and threaded, you find yourself together making verbal patterns,

visual attachments, which you can't unless willing
an escape. If you compere, all concepts can be made concrete,
released suddenly, a movement in commonplace, maybe over

your head. Like I've been searching suddenly all over
for justification. Dicing through bends in the time.
It's suddenly a wall of laughter – warping occasion

on a determined fault line. Or, we are all attached
    anyway.
Not the same as attack. Bent on understanding,
see? It will curve us as we lean it out. The response

which was so automated, so confused, is more like
keeping up chance, smirched now in the
temperature of the room. High order, it was heady

lately. You had to be there to experience. And even though

one left early, odd throbbing away, ready to hatch.
And though you lay your ear very close to the side of it,

which side have you taken? Responsive or servile?
Others' needs don't curb in the place used to blast
others' intentions for. Can it be generous while qualifying

embrace? The area is warm where thought pounds on it,
day after day, bending pale green shade afterwards.
That's unclear. Or maybe the eye which makes light of or sense
anyway.

When Expectation Relinquishes Underneath Itself

in concentric myth-lines.   Formal the plot –
not deleteriousness.   You expect forward motion.

To act –   not just in a field –
but over a field.   In it,
heading out,   spreading.
Plotting one's course beside familiars.
Perhaps rendered, getting a taxi
                 or plane.

There in reversible relation
are more fields – consciousness permits. Grounds for ill-feeling,
due to closeness. The heroine of a book mirroring a complex
(disconcerting)! You're due certain erasures,
and for courage read luck.

   Untold properties push you outward. Messages will not bear you
   though masquerade readiness.

In the morning,
more seething than usual,   because seeming uncertain,
sleep is doled out – whimsical – by the hour.
Smell of barbarism each time   put to the unconscious.

Describe – briefly – her lips. But cannot.
  Only parallels emerge – peccadilloes. And careless attentions.
These always – but they can't, namely – control measures.

Microscopically viable. Lingering over   real joints –
visible to the few.   Over like coloured rows. The two parts
heady in contrast.

Live transmission of a calf muscle   being   segregated –
literally   torn apart –   placated.
  Or unconsciousness (parades).   But there is no such thing.

By remembrance I mean:
always exceeding the mark.
Rows disjointed like heads,   automatically piled.
Not even cheap
but free, biting the point, as if to enlarge it.

What was it that first got away? What muscles left that are moving?
Are all the returns fervent /
trenchantly uninformed.

  Con amore? Or could that tell when it was "broken."
So much morality

drenching the lost production.

There were dialogues, but they were interested / bougie, with no matter but
who   re-settling   all scenic routes   this way   & flawed.

   I realized that what made us happy contravened
   ourselves. Prepared armament. Remembrance.

And once you're not happy   – I will have gone.   Or conversely,
once I've gone   – you won't have noticed me. Or your freedom.

Regrets shaded from exactly this distance, so prompt a release.

And why should we want to grip onto
that unfinished scene.

OF ALL THE SURPRISES: A LOVE POEM FOR SEATON
(DUSIE, 2007)

Of all the surprises
that least expected

anyway between real
fixtures

(which for months now, almost
worked out of the system)

when I'd say to myself
(before almost verbally)

there's nothing to build to-
ward & least of all specially.

When I least thought it
& had nothing to argue with

(remorselessly,
                indiscriminately)

assumed nothing but —
shocked offering as if —

out of azure blindness of —
beyond what happened —

without explanation.
                Because love

across love
                having nothing

but love
         here because.

10 or 12 times
I picture you up

& forget how it is
because incongruity

is north of permanence
& the optimum mix

is really something
(frequently distracting).

When I do it is for
getting.

Because love
so except

when it least
begets —

more so.
I long(ed) for you

& as luck wld also love
as much as this

after
words.

(Meanwhile language is
astonishing facets

almost comes near
a not-too-extensive

feelings themselves.
It can never be too —

its spatial properties
are many & varied:

discontinuous
                / new.)

Suddenly, shockingly
you make me see through

as if all my faults
as if love

splayed
sudden —

As if for you —
These speculative fantasies

couple with real physical
when we're together

can barely monitor —
Delays our leitmotifs

that pausing incongruous.
Are you always the same?

(…We are always partial.)
I long excessively

   to scratch you again
& pull you close

   your cuteness bangs
wow, but for I love

   in it where I love
because nothing

   but love
because & for you.

from WHEN I SAY I BELIEVE WOMEN
(BAD PRESS, 2007)

When I say I believe women & men read &
write differently I mean that women & men
read & write pretty differently. Whether this is
biologically 'essential' or just straightforward
like when you left the toaster burning or
because women have a subordinated
relationship to power in their guts I don't
know. Is this clear enough for you to follow. I
don't know. When I say we should try not to
forget the author, this is because that would be
bad manners as well as ridiculous. When I say
there is a centre into which exclusion bends I
mean *nothing*. When I hear you ask how much
money did you get or how far have you got
into your work, something internal plunges for
the exit, like puking, it wants to get out -
because you're *still* being hostile (after all
these years) - & look toward the charcoaled
meats for rescue. There they are still on fire.

When I read your attempts at Latin & 'cum' & humour I think: no one cares about you after 1 a.m. &: it's so exhausting, &: did your father(s) never tell you to "stop showing off to people." Were you never crushed & leant on by another? I guess that's why my weariness comes from & distends. Or perhaps it's just obvious bad manners. When I get excited because I think, why should I hide the fact? Does that mean I have loose morals or absence (social awareness) or cool. I will pretend from now on. When I lose heart because there are too too many 'I's for my liking, & you won't write to me these days because you say I lost heart too many times, & that's ridiculous, but OK, because you're *still* hostile after all these years that are still there smouldering.

Sometimes seems to serve pretty obviously for exclusion & showoffs Or tumbleweed arranging So many times good women have written to me saying they can't subscribe not really out of shyness but rather "find i want to have something specific to *say and too often feel i don't have something spot-on to add right when it's needed" I wonder a lot of the men don't seem to have this inclination Might call it modesty or else losing heart

Whenever I write *you* it blends & morphs into so many others. That's what comes from being informal I guess. Or not cool. Or erotic. When I get respite from absence, when I think about SPACE - annihilating all that's made... I don't know about presence (metaphysically), I never felt any. When that's all corrupt-ridiculous, a dream-trampling, I hear that Dundee's a satellite of Cambridge, I laugh & puke & think how nice to be a lesbian putting on plays by Olson. When I watch films with '70s headscarves on heroes like they were the good old days.[11] (But free love comes at a price, at least the cost of one or two burnt fingers.) Our mothers learnt that for us amongst nothing.

Wrote how terrified we were about the ongoing destruction of green spaces in England How it made you just want to 'get out'

Certainly where I grew up reading ~~Marvell~~ is being lost & overdeveloped & What would ~~C. Olson~~ make of such greenbelt catastrophe

---

[1] Shocked & surprised at the physical difference between say ~~Klute ('71) & Alex in Wonderland ('70)~~ Especially in that scene with his friend where they're talking about how his woman's a bad lay

Always shocked &
surprised at how regularly
you put yourself 'forward'
& self-advertise Especially
when I think about Carla
Harryman, Kathleen Fraser,
Leslie Scalapino How
they try to avoid "fitting
the radical object into the
square peg of patriarchal
canon-making narratives"
'Women's Writing: Hybrid
Thoughts on Contingent
Hierarchies and Reception,'
1999

Because yes there were a lot
of things that were difficult
& not even that constructive
to follow (I find this about
academe generally)

The SPACE allowed around each satellite, you
want to crush it & plunge into an abyss of
your own name, obviously-shaped through the
light, even though self-naming is a fault &
way too semantic. Whenever you talk the
people salivate; others write "pretentious
bullshit" in the margins, underscored &
overlined with envy or malice or maybe just
obvious good sense. The pockets are full of
stones. When people hear you talk they think:
you've got a way with yourself - or: if it were
me I'd run - or: words. Or: way too erotic.
When I say lips like chances are the keys to all
surface like a true domestic animal, you
should see into my room, I haven't vacuumed
in days. There is almost no SPACE left.

What elements are in the vowel-sounds of
your mouth, too recent like carbon rings.[1]
Anyone can tell the interrogative is a style like
any other (apron). I'm wondering about
nursing & cooking & following you round,
wiping the saliva from your tongue. That body
more prompted like recent words dressed up in
a foul mouth that wonders about illuminating
gaps: no money, real work or outlets, just an
object which heeds, a verb without status.
Daughter's inconsequence unloosed on a
whole crowd of informals to no (obvious)
purpose.

Who just recently 'flipped out' as Scalapino would say & got committed There are so many things he could have said & done which has taken a lot of time ~~to put into this bag of nerves~~

~~I've been carrying around with me ever since~~

---

[1] Rosmarie Waldrop: "When I say I believe that women have a
soul and that its substance contains two carbon rings the picture in
the foreground makes it difficult to find its application," *Lawn of
Excluded Middle*, 11

That uninhibited experience told the time &
your temperature without difficulty. There was

Didn't know what it had
meant It was only then you
got me thinking who'd had
no long-term aim at all but
~~nonetheless found it~~
~~hurtful you could just up &~~
~~leave like that~~

no object to my supposing, but a verb with no
status. When you told me to take it any way I
wanted, I took it in the best sense possible. I
guess that wasn't what you meant me to do. No
object, no money, & no outlets. Woman's a

In Paris this guy who'd
watched me eat my
floating island dessert
alone He'd ~~said he liked~~
~~women who looked lost~~
~~& thought I could do with~~
~~the company~~

floating island round an imperfectly-baked
dessert. In an oven you get burnt. Is this too
obvious are you getting warm or even angry.
This isn't metaphorical, I mean it to be *true
statements*, shook up like inside hurt. However
you decide to take them. Do I look like I'm
joking when I tell you that "The meaning of
certainty is getting burned."[1]

---

[1] Rosmarie Waldrop, *Lawn of Excluded Middle*, 18

I once said you were the emery board to my fantasy, the CO2 to my fire. In late adolescence you were pushed forward, they said your will was 'atypical.' I knew the main points. Implicit in all this was a fatal altering, in spite of rigour, succinct but weighed on. It was helpful to take a little series of pills in place of you. Set down precedence of mighty but unsure chemical reliance. Elements not scheduled. Arisen not meeting. A flame who plunged into defunct night help me to float down shaken but deserving no less than everything.

The hostile space around each name beckons.
I would long to work on soundly besides. Who
plunged into the night. At that time deserving
no less than everything. Finally, I come to
visit you with your slow gaze & deliberate
blindsight. Your hair which was always fine is
streaked with grey & adequate silence. No
adapting, just a process unravelling itself
soundly here in other people's minds. But they
say nothing can grow beneath greatness
anyway - the pastoral typifies - nothing can
not get burnt. Anything shades up to
difference or gradates nicely. I have not
reached this stage for nothing. But not even
now, completely wilful.[1] *When I say women
don't need that kind of hurt for anything I
mean it* not even as a way of joking.

Seeing you there has been some of the worst times of my life I wish I could get ~~knowledge of insanity~~ out of my head

Or else you think someone's pretending to be me which is so hurtful Your obstinacy is so hurtful when reality's obvious

---

[1] ~~I wish I could get you out of my head~~

Dear America

That courage sliding toward uncertain luck / will (it) must have
(been) taken. Not achievement, but a sort of (ill) defined rejection
of normal positions. Don't push it, I have nothing but used-up
humour, (zero) expectancy. If you find yourself (here) again I will
have torched it (then). You're (not) the only one to have thought
(of), but most of us reckon with the layers (of) placing, society's
sedimentation, & a world without those seems terrifying vacant?
Such an extreme journey as you (must) have (had) leaves glowing
but futile. No wonder the fog & (the) oil skies & carves you (up)
now. It will do worse as time (collects). Or, even those vagaries
don't have to be (destructive) widowed. Relational aspects are what
(most) people value (most), not scorn from emptying the world
around them (via an accumulation). That history you've (mis)taken
for a gaudy entrance, welcoming into the fold(s) deviants. Patched
up by stone, plyed as with marble well, who else, (but) everyone
figured. While how (you) long fucking the skies your elation's
turned all of it (similar) on but with TV & eyes & is twisted.

The sense of falling

Apart metaphor.

Know how to do.

Push texture.

Think: you is to formal what length is to time allotted.

Imagine electrifying.

Imagine sequencing (semi-unconscious).

Go 'smack' in the middle.

Leave unprepared error.

Think: early on in the life my guess is precisely that. Later we learn
it instinctively, our terror doubles.

Remember the moment when you uttered straight by yourself.

Remember your good will & the gap between it.

Imagine how worked at this analogous question: when the door opened, its stench hit me a metal sky.

When I was in with you as if we didn't have to talk.

When you were at disappointment, your chair couldn't keep still.

Like we didn't have the right tools to communicate (on).

So pushed up texture toward the code.

& leant back structure. The fall came down to our ears.

About here.

In translation

It's the open sky with
its blue voltage made me do it.

It's a horizon again, not spectral, but
to-the-point minute. This almost
uncertainly provocative
is like quasi-private attachment.

Where you might have said 'crack open,'
    we want to break.
Where you might have said 'indifferent,'
    meaning no harm.

It's because permanently
substantive this
Greek orienting.

Is it a naming thing?

Clusters swallow.
The foothills of light penetrative.
What lizard –

are you clearing
into the space below my foot.

It's waters' iridescent
mimesis.

The blueness survives but
never a support network.

Struck so clearly from above,
it had Greek blood too. I arranged myself
according to your wants:
a matter of each pulse
attenuating.

That's the Spartan
in us both. Where's my
armoury?

In this world

Is the distinction that a collage is more artificial than a sex doll?
Is that painful copying the template of your mind.
What activity, if you swim naked, does that make you a free
    citizen?
When can resistance be satisfying even when it means you have no
    original.
One of your tricks is to impose your own mind on your years;
I've noticed that.
No one's responsible for those choices. A lost year in a hotel in
    broad daylight.
Why is it disjunctive remembering your holding the girl till her
    anger was not mollified.
Why the restatement, have you pervaded what fears.
Will she be reinstated whenever you make love to a new tradition.
That is, placing your barriers, or at least, removing them equally, in
    that particular pile.
The actual conversations we had were not about content.
The actual conversations took place somewhere different: stylistics.
How can you not see I am altogether not shirking intentions.
There is this underwritten suppression, it clamps us with its
    concrete teeth.
How can you not see I am petrified whose eyes were mistranslated
    by the English. Translate that into the typeface. Even music has
    its rewards.
Even a simple sentence can hold enough water to flood a museum.
I just want you to look inside my sea-scape until you see Nereids.
I just want endless passion & the imprint of someone till I'm not a

sex doll with a PhD.

I just want it to be redone over & over till it's perfect.

I just want syntactical impermanence, readjusted perspectives &
your revolutionary propensities.

I just want I just want I just want

from HOW TO MAKE MILLIONS
(AREHOUSE, 2005)

Your revenue body brings superlux
trash piece

changes in

circumspect.

Well doesn't feeling the preference unite

flighty at 2 am as smooth as paper is
toward breath fountain. As it

untold as founded
leaning
presses.

Whereas formal shapes realize
&
opulent fall.

expense stretching Europe
view-taker surmounts
That's it.

We untie
          Paper as flowers ripped for

centre-fold.
malleable showing.

When it returns will be   months gaudy,
but venue is on unknown   free
still obelisk.

Mouth for displaying
obscenity feedback   &

instant re-

phrased   sound

gratified.

Sound on the end of a

paper.
Depending on   *cuts that I do*   *&*
mouth a lot

Happy [not enervated]

They think,   seeing dark tips on the cloud lining,
several to make up day.

          Past particle
is what, pastiche summer –

or variegated line endings –
It is not coming toward
circling.

          Always creases
up certain hitches.
          Then spell   n e r v y
          out
. Formal.

          Otherwise inattention.
Isn't that natural only.
Speaking as what's whole.

          Then said to him about
certain purpose.
With the skin open / shocked
systems.   Travelling round this area.

          City a bag of
nerve endings.

from THE DIRT GLITCH LAND ALTER AFFAIR
(AREHOUSE, 2004)

---

*Not misrepresenting but even producing & being produced by
its very nature*

Like   movement on a big screen,
this   thing   being   separate   then

meaning as a consequence of something.
This thing we started to do
         when dreamt: "Who was going to shoot up"
& woke?   With his hand dipping in fog   SAYING

Images de Paris. Image in   something (copy), or else

a great tract. The rueful fallen   "Will the day tell someone"?
& this thing,   you have a complex   on it,
might not be any kind of construction.

                              So the dazed fallen
all about should see   shatterless improvements? Collapsed
perspective?

Down the Boulevard with him   – in orange –   &
a funny hat   &

The other night when I was sleeping,
with his hand wrapped round pathos –   repeating
all the crap that merges – the criticism –
open-eyed & wider
,imperceptibly,
like bystanders, though transparent, it was

the same emotional-hanger-on
            slipping from the apartment unheard.

While this thing could not regenerate   much.
Everything   leading   to impressions
– sordid Hollywood-dreams –
faked row of stuccoes,
formless glass mess behind the museum.

                              But the real
has mud [on its]   hands,   comes societally unprepared,

produces code-governed warnings   something
            screening   whole profundities in fog.
Really startled,   really now, the movement of sight clam-
bering to
an archetype.   Will not succumb so easily, will
not
fall off
            where everything's diminished in it, not so facilitated or by
            you but him.

(Re.vision)

That is how progress. That is wine settling
toward taking its place. The vast limping, throat at your tiller.
Land where future machinery palls irrespective
and at the side of major authority brains perpetual delirium.

That is not what I meant progress. I who argued for I to extinguish
the sun in midst of zinc, etymologize hardly, print out manically
all the marginalized errors. Mine not yours / hers / his / its, etc.

Your supporters on crutches, your cerebral cortex speeding
on floating hammers. Remove that masses and come sit.
I want your title, address, wristwatch & everything else
you see tensely. A sideline's possible. Then mounting objectives
take optimism, strangulate, it is all on outside.